Payment Systems and Funds Transfer Activities

Comptroller's Handbook

Narrative and Procedures - March 1990

Comptroller of the Currency
Administrator of National Banks

Payment Systems and Funds Transfer Activities (Section 410)

Table of Contents

Payment Systems and Funds Transfer Activities (Section 410)   Introduction

Financial institutions and their customers are recognizing a growing need to manage cash resources more efficiently. Economic and financial factors, together with improved data communications and computer technology, have increased demand for electronic funds transfer (EFT) services from the financial industry. EFT is defined as: any transfer of funds which is initiated through an electronic terminal, telephonic instrument, computer, or magnetic tape so as to order, instruct, or authorize a financial institution to debit or credit an account.

The volume of funds and securities exchanged daily through the electronic funds transfer systems is in the trillions of dollars. For U.S. financial institutions, these transactions are handled by wholesale or large dollar systems such as FedWire, CHIPS, and SWIFT. Additionally, other funds transfer services, such as Automated Clearing Houses (ACH), Automated Teller Machines (ATM), Point-of-Sale (POS) systems, telephone bill paying, home banking systems, debit cards, and "smart cards" are gaining widespread customer use. Many of these transactions are initiated by customers rather than financial institutions. These are normally considered retail funds transfer systems. Financial institutions and regulatory authorities should be concerned with the quality of internal controls and management's awareness of the inherent risks associated with the various systems.

Purposes and Functions of the Payment Systems

A system of payments is an essential element of any economy. The system must be able to communicate information about individual transfers of funds and settle the actual transfers. Settlement means the receipt by the payee's depository institution of acceptable final funds, which irrevocably extinguish the obligation of the payor's depository institution. Settlement can occur on a "gross" basis, in which each transfer is settled individually, or periodically on a "net" basis, in which credits and debits can offset each other. In the United States, the overall payments system consists of a number of individual payments mechanisms. Together, they make up the system for transmitting payments information and for transferring funds and securities from one party to another.

Large-Dollar Electronic Funds Transfer Systems

Although several different mechanisms make up the U.S. payments system, most of the dollar value of all funds transfers and much of the associated risk is concentrated in two electronic systems used principally to transfer large-dollar payments between banks, FedWire, and CHIPS.

FedWire

FedWire, operated by the Federal Reserve, allows any depository institution with a Federal Reserve account to transfer funds from that account to the Federal Reserve account of any other depository institution. The operating rules of FedWire, covered under Regulation J of the Board of Governors, provide that each transfer is final and irrevocable when a receiving depository institution is notified of it. Thus, a depository institution receiving a FedWire transfer is not exposed to any credit risk from the sending depository institution, nor does it normally bear any credit risk in making the proceeds of the transfer immediately available to a customer. The Reserve banks provide the intraday credit needed to handle the dollar volumes processed each day on FedWire by allowing depository institutions to initiate FedWire transfers that may exceed, at a given moment, the balance in their reserve or clearing accounts. These intraday overdrafts of accounts are referred to as "daylight overdrafts." The Reserve bank—not the receiving depository institution—is exposed to the risk that the sending institution will be unable to deposit sufficient funds in its account to cover the transfers. The operation of the FedWire systems is, thus, based on the provision of liquidity, and the absorption of the resulting risk, by the public sector.

CHIPS

The other major payments mechanism—in terms of the dollar value of transfers processed—is the Clearing House Interbank Payments System (CHIPS) in New York, operated by the New York Clearing House Association. In this system, information about individual transfers is exchanged by the participating depository institutions throughout the day. At the end of the day, the value of all transfers sent and received by each of the participants is totaled and netted to determine a net credit or debit position for each participant. The institutions participating in CHIPS are divided into two categories: "settling participants" (numbering 21) and "other" (118). Institutions in the larger groups settle their net activity for the day with a designated settling participant. Settling participants are responsible for their own net positions and the net positions of the institutions that they represent in the settlement. Settlement among the settling participants is accomplished through a settlement account on the books of the Federal Reserve Bank of New York: Settling participants in a net debit position make FedWire transfers into the settlement account equal to their net debit positions. Thus, CHIPS is settled on a same-day, net basis but only at the close of business.

In contrast to FedWire, in which the public sector provides liquidity, CHIPS creates interbank credit exposures among the system's participants. Once a depository institution enters information about a transfer into the system, it cannot subsequently rescind the transfer; nonetheless, settlement for the transfer—the actual transfer of account balances—does not occur until the end of the day. At any time during the course of the day, some CHIPS participants will have initiated transfers with total dollar value greater than that of the transfers they have received. These participants, that are in a net debit position, are essentially receiving intraday credit from the participants that have received transfers with a total value higher than that of the transfers they have sent. The aggregate amount of intraday credit extended to facilitate the operation of the FedWire and CHIPS systems for funds transfer is enormous, averaging about $90 billion per day.

Institutional Practices on FedWire and CHIPS

Banks and other depository institutions use these large-dollar payments mechanisms both to transfer funds related to their own operations—for example, federal funds transactions—and to transfer funds on behalf of their customers. The flow of funds associated with these activities is extremely large compared with the reserve and clearing account balances that represent the payments system's ultimate base of liquidity. The implied velocity of these balances, which has increased significantly in recent years, and the volume of activity on FedWire and CHIPS have made intraday credit an essential element in the smooth functioning of both of these systems.

The types of transactions giving rise to the majority of transfers differ between

FedWire and CHIPS. Surveys suggest that roughly one-third of the activity, that is, number of transactions, on FedWire is federal funds transactions and one-fourth is securities transactions. The next largest category of FedWire activity, commercial transactions, is about one-fifth of the total. In contrast, roughly two-thirds of the activity and nearly one-half the dollar value of the activity on CHIPS is foreign-exchange transactions. Another one-fourth of the activity and one-third of the dollar value is Eurodollar placements. Thus, the most significant types of transactions on the two systems overlap little. Virtually all transactions involving foreign exchange are handled through CHIPS, and virtually all transactions involving the purchase, redemption, or financing of securities and derivative instruments, as well as federal funds, are handled on FedWire.

Society for Worldwide Interbank Financial Telecommunications (SWIFT)

SWIFT, wire transfer message system, was formed in 1973 by approximately 240 of the largest European and North American banks as a private telecommunications network. The SWIFT network provides user banks with a private international communications link among themselves. Security of the messages in the system is assured by encryption of all data. However, telecommunications between user banks and the SWIFT network may not be encrypted. Other security features include log-on and log-off controls, message sequence controls, and a highly structured format for text messages. In addition to customer and bank funds transfers, SWIFT is used to transmit foreign exchange confirmations, debit and credit entry confirmations, statements, collections, and documentary credits. Each SWIFT country has its own internal organization. Most countries have a national group that meets regularly to review system operations and recommend appropriate modifications. Each member bank pays a one-time admittance fee. Shares in SWIFT are distributed according to the volume of messages transmitted by each member.

Payment System Risk

Payment system risk refers to the risk of financial loss to providers and users of payment-system services and their creditors. Such risk arises from the extension of unsecured, intraday credit to facilitate the transmission of payment messages or funds. These transmissions often arise from an underlying exchange of financial instruments or of real goods and services.

The volume of intraday credit related to transfer of funds and book-entry securities, on large-dollar payments networks alone, has grown to more than $130 billion daily. The Federal Reserve is a major unsecured creditor. Daylight overdrafts of reserve accounts due to funds transfers average more than $60 billion daily, and overdrafts due to book-entry transactions contribute nearly as much to Federal Reserve exposures. Because these credit extensions are at risk, the Federal Reserve and ultimately the taxpayer stand to lose considerable sums if debtors fail to meet their obligations. Private participants in the payments system also experience large credit-risk exposures. On CHIPS, the major private payments system, such credit extensions approach $50 billion. Many other formal and less formal payments mechanisms also create intraday credit, such as offshore dollar-clearing systems or bilateral correspondent relationships. The failure of even one major participant to meet its payments obligations in these private arrangements could create a systemic disruption of the payments system or of financial markets generally.

Overall credit risk in the payments system thus has three components: (1) direct credit risk to the Federal Reserve—the possibility that a borrowing institution may be unable to cover its intraday overdraft arising from a transfer of funds or receipt of book-entry securities and thus cause the Federal Reserve Banks to incur a loss, (2) private direct credit risk—the possibility of loss to institutions extending daylight credit as the result of the borrowing institution's inability to cover its intraday debit position for reasons independent of developments in the payments system, and (3) systemic risk—the possibility of loss to a series of creditors arising from the inability of one borrowing institution to cover its intraday debit position to one or more private creditor institutions.

Credit Risks

Sender Risk

Sender risk is the risk a depository assumes when it makes an irrevocable payment on behalf of a customer through an extension of credit. Credit can be extended explicitly, by granting a loan, or implicitly, by paying against uncollected or provisional funds or against insufficient balances.

Receiver Risk

Receiver risk involves risk to an institution upon acceptance of funds from the sender. This may be a customer, another institution, or the payments system. As the receiver of funds, an institution must rely on the sender's ability to settle its obligations at the end of day. Receiver risk is present when payments are revocable within the system until final settlement.

Settlement Risks

Settlement risk concerns whether each participant in the system will be able to honor their obligations at time of settlement. If one participant fails to settle, this may disrupt settlement for other participants. As a result, the system's settlement fails. This also is referred to as liquidity risk. Like receiver risk, settlement risk is present when payments are conditional or revocable until final settlement. Settlement risk also is an exposure subject to operational disruptions or sovereign actions.

Systemic Risks

Systemic risk is an outgrowth of settlement risk. The failure of one participant to settle deprives other institutions of expected funds and, in turn, prevents those institutions from settling. To the extent that chains of obligations develop, it is possible for a participant doing no business at all with a failed institution to suffer because of the effect of the failed institution on an intermediate participant and its ability to settle.

Legal Risks

Any transaction occurring in a payments system is subject to the interpretation of courts in different countries and legal systems. This issue is normally addressed by the adoption of "governing law" provisions in the rules of the systems themselves. These provide for all disputes between members to be settled under the laws of a specific jurisdiction. However, they may be of limited value if a local court refuses to recognize the jurisdiction of a foreign court. This risk is difficult to address because there is no binding system of international commercial law for electronic payments. Banks should seek legal opinion regarding the enforceability of transactions settled through a particular system.

Sovereign Risks

Sovereign risk applies to all types of payments systems. It is the risk that action by a government may affect either a system or particular participants in a system. This action could be detrimental to other participants in the system. An example of this risk would be the imposition of exchange control regulations on a bank participating in international foreign exchange activities. While the bank itself may be both willing and able to settle its position, government intervention prevents it from doing so. This risk can be controlled by monitoring a bank's exposure to counterparties located in nations where this type of action is considered possible.

Operational Risks

Operational risks include:

- System Failure—caused by a breakdown in the hardware and/or software supporting the system. This may result from design defects, insufficient system capacity to handle transaction volumes, or mechanical breakdown, including telecommunications.

- System Disruption—the system is unavailable to process transactions. This may be caused by system failure, destruction of the facility (natural disasters, fires, terrorism), or operation shutdown (employee actions, business failure, or government action).

- System Compromise—resulting from fraud, malicious damage to data, or error.

The loss of availability of the payment system from whatever source can adversely affect major participants, their correspondents, markets, and interdependent networks.

Operational risks should be controlled by the banks through a sound system of internal controls including physical security, date security, systems testing, segregations of duties, backup systems, and contingency planning. In addition, a comprehensive audit program to assess risks, adequacy of controls, and compliance with bank policies is essential.

Since most banks are third-party participants in international networks, their ability to influence controls is limited. Nevertheless, they must recognize risks to their own business operations and compensate through their own internal controls. In addition, banks should exercise their influence over third- party systems to the extent possible to insist upon sound operations for system continuity and integrity.

Control Issues

Management needs to consider and resolve numerous issues when participating in payment systems. These issues are generally the same for both national and international systems.

Guidelines should consider:

- Controls to reduce sender and receiver risks. These should include:
  - Bilateral credit limits.
  - Debit cap limits, including a process to determine these limits.
  - A process to monitor and control these limits on a real-time basis.

- Controls to limit the overall exposure of the system, including debit cap limits.

- Requirements to ensure that settlement occurs. This should address:
  - the conditions for settlement such as location, time, and settling procedures.
  - the type of settlement (i.e., provisionality or finality of payment).
  - the guarantor(s), if any, of payment finality. This may involve a central bank, the system owner/operator, and/or the system participants.
  - the basis for providing necessary liquidity to the system. This may require allocation of funding by participants, coinsurance, or central bank guarantees.

- Legal issues governing the system operation, including local laws, business practices, and government regulation.

- Capabilities of the system and the bank to handle emergency situations. This may require backup operations or the ability for the bank to bypass the network.

- Responsibility for reviewing the bank's participation in payment systems.

Payments Risk Reduction Program

In 1986, the Federal Reserve System implemented the Risk Reduction Program. The program is aimed at controlling the levels of intraday credit exposure on large-dollar U.S. payments systems, including FedWire and private-sector systems, and encouraging depository institutions to exercise better control over such credit exposure. The basic objectives are to ensure the continuing smooth operations of the payments system and to limit the systemic risk implications of a credit shock to the payments system.

As a primary means for improved management of credit exposures in the payments mechanism, the program encourages participating depository institutions to set a series of limits or caps on various aspects of intraday credit exposure. This includes caps related to exposure on private-sector systems, such as CHIPS, as well as a cross-system, net-debit cap, which establishes a maximum for an institution's total net-debit position across all large-dollar payments systems (i.e., CHIPS and FedWire) at any one time during the business day. The cross-system cap, which is set at a multiple of capital, is based on an institution's self-evaluation of creditworthiness, operational controls, and credit policies and procedures.

In accordance with the policy statement, the self-assessment and cap selection should be annually documented, reviewed, and approved by the institution's board of directors. A copy of the "Self-Assessment Review" is contained in the Appendix. In lieu of the self-assessment process and selection of a sender net-debit cap, an institution's board may annually approve a "de minimis cap," which represents the lesser of 20 percent of capital or $500,000. An institution should report its cap to its reserve bank, which will monitor the bank's net debit positions on an ex post, or after the fact, basis. Local reserve banks will provide management reports to each institution and to its primary supervisory agency.

The policy directly affects only those institutions that participate in private wire-transfer systems (e.g., CHIPS) and/or that incur "daylight overdrafts" on FedWire.

Policy

The OCC has committed to cooperate with the Federal Reserve in supervising the Payments System Risk Reduction program. As the primary regulator of national banks, it is our responsibility to identify and supervise those institutions that are at risk or that pose a risk to the system because of their participation in a large-dollar wire transfer system. The supervisory objectives in implementing the PSR program are:

- To identify national banks that pose risks to the payments system, and
- To determine national bank compliance with the program.

National banks will require supervisory attention when they:

- Incur daylight overdrafts and have not established a net- debit cap or a de minimis cap with a Federal Reserve Bank.
- Establish a cap that appears to be too high.
- Exceed their established cap frequently.
- Experience a decline in performance (i.e., deteriorating CAMEL rating or adverse economic impact).

All supervisory information regarding national bank compliance with the PSR program should be communicated to the Federal Reserve on a frequent and timely basis.

Procedures

PSR must be considered when developing the supervisory strategy for each national bank. A bank is expected to participate in the PSR program if:

- the bank participates in a private wire-transfer system, and/or
- the bank incurs daylight overdrafts on FedWire.

If the bank is expected to participate in the program, then its supervisory strategy should consider:

- Has the bank established a sender net-debit cap or a de minimis cap with its Federal Reserve Bank?
- Is the self-assessment annually reviewed and the cap approved by the bank's board of directors, or is a de minimis cap annually approved by the board?
- Does the cap appear to appropriately limit the amount of credit risk that this bank presents to the nation's payments system?
- Does use of the cap pose a threat to the safety and soundness of the national bank?

Appropriate supervisory action should be planned based on the preliminary analysis of the national bank's need to participate in the program, its level of compliance, and any potential risk to safety and soundness. These procedures may be used as a tool to review national bank compliance when further analysis is required.

Comments regarding a bank's non-compliance with the PSR program should be communicated to the supervised institution and the district office in accordance with district guidelines. The district office liaison will communicate with the Federal Reserve to the extent necessary.

Select from among the following Tier I and Tier II examination procedures those steps necessary to evaluate the funds transfer activities of the bank.

Tier I

1. As part of the examination planning function, determine through the District liaison whether the bank incurs daylight overdrafts on the FedWire system and the level of those overdrafts.

2. Does the institution:

    a. incur daylight overdrafts on FedWire, and/or

    b. participate in a private wire-transfer system?

3. If the answer to both of the above questions is no, there is no need to perform any additional procedures. If the answer to either of the above questions is yes, then complete Tiers I and/or II as necessary.

4. Review the bank's internal controls, policies, practices, and procedures for ensuring/monitoring compliance with the Federal Reserve Bank's guidelines, and determine:

    a. Has the board of directors adopted written policies and procedures that are adequate in scope?

    b. Are existing policies adequately disseminated to individuals affected?

    c. Has the bank established an employee training program to ensure that applicable employees have the knowledge necessary to ensure compliance with the program?

d. Do management information systems provide timely and accurate data to enable personnel to make informed decisions?

e. Has management established adequate reporting systems to keep the board of directors or a committee thereof appropriately informed?

5. Review the work of the internal/external auditors and/or compliance officer as it relates to PSR, and determine:

a. Is PSR reviewed?

b. Is the function adequate in terms of:

- Independence?
- Scope?
- Coverage?
- Frequency of review?

c. Do bank management and the board of directors institute corrective action to address deficiencies noted by the audit and/or compliance functions?

6. Has the bank established a sender net debit cap or a de minimis cap with its Federal Reserve Bank?

a. For institutions with a de minimis cap, proceed to step 7.

b. For institutions that have performed a self-assessment, proceed to step 8.

c. For institutions that have not established a cap, proceed to step 3.

7. For institutions which have established a de minimis cap:

a. Do board of directors' minutes reflect consideration of the Federal Reserve's PSR policy and how it applies to their institution?

b. Did the board of directors approve a de minimis cap on the institution's cross-system funds overdrafts?

    c. Has the board of directors submitted a copy of the certification of the de minimis cap to its Federal Reserve Bank within the past 12 months?

    d. Can the institution monitor its payment activity for daylight overdrafts and, if necessary, on a cross-system basis?

    e. Are controls in place to keep the institution from exceeding its funds overdraft cap?

    f. Are the controls effective?

    g. Does the institution use daylight overdrafts only on an occasional basis?

    h. Has the board of directors considered implementing a self-assessment review if the institution consistently incurs daylight overdrafts or exceeds its de minimis cap limit?

    i. Judging from the results of the overall examination, is the institution considered creditworthy in terms of its intraday borrowing?

    j. When the de minimis cap procedures are completed, proceed to step 9.

8. The following procedures are for institutions that have established a sender net debit cap through the self-assessment process.

    a. Does the bank's self-assessment file contain adequate documentation addressing all components? (See Self-assessment Review section)

    b. Does the file indicate annual updates of the self-assessments and reports submitted to the board of directors detailing those updates?

    c. Do the board minutes reflect adequate review by the directorate of self-assessment requirements at least annually?

d. Do the board minutes reflect board of directors' consideration of issues surrounding the matter?

e. Do the board minutes reflect review of correspondence or counseling efforts by the Federal Reserve or other supervisory agency?

f. Does the formal board resolution establishing the institution's cap identify the following:

- The rating for each of the three separate rating components?
- The institution's overall rating?

g. Do the board minutes reflect the board of directors' review of whether the institution is subject to the limitations on inter-affiliate transfers? If applicable:

- Do the minutes indicate approval of specific intraday credit limits for each affiliate within the last 12 months?
- Has a copy of the resolution been sent to the Federal Reserve Bank?

h. If the board has decided that the institution is not subject to the limitation on inter-affiliate transfers and there are affiliate banks:

- Does the institution frequently incur daylight overdrafts?
- Are the size, timing, and duration of the overdrafts fairly consistent, and do they correlate with the initiation of transfers to affiliates?
- Does the institution regularly send one or more large transfers (in relation to its capital) to an affiliate(s), other than those on behalf of customers, and receive offsetting transfers later in the day?

i. If the answers to all the questions in (h) are yes, then there should be a presumption that the daylight overdraft policy's limitations on inter-affiliate transactions apply to the transfer being sent by the institution to its affiliates.

- Discuss with management why it is felt that the limitations do not apply.
- Consult with the Reserve Bank concerning the applicability of the limitations on inter-affiliate transfers.

9. Review the results of Tier I. If the systems and controls (including audit and/or compliance officer functions) are inadequate, weak, or nonexistent in any area, proceed to the applicable sections of Tier II.

Tier II

1. Complete or update the Module A of the Internal Control Questionnaire.

2. Based upon an evaluation of internal controls and work performed by internal/external auditor (see separate program), determine the scope of the examination.

3. Test for compliance with policies, practices, procedures, and internal controls in conjunction with performing the remaining examination procedures. Also, obtain a listing of any deficiencies noted in the latest review done by internal/external auditors from the examiner assigned "Internal and External Audits," and determine whether appropriate corrections have been made.

4. Complete or update Module B of the Internal Control Questionnaire to evaluate risks resulting from payments made against insufficient funds or credits extended in the form of intraday or overnight overdrafts. Review for:

   a. Established limits, and frequency and scope of internal credit reviews.

   b. Reporting and approval procedures for payments released in excess of established limits.

   c. Compliance with intraday overdraft limits and approval and reporting requirements.

   d. Analysis of the creditworthiness of borrowers with overnight overdrafts in excess of the credit line. (The credit evaluation procedure is the same as that applied to any other form of short-term credit.)

5. Perform appropriate verification procedures.

6. Obtain or construct an organizational chart and flowchart for the wire transfer area, and determine job responsibilities and flow of work through that department.

7. Review the bank's standard form or other written agreements with its customers and vendors, and determine whether those agreements clearly define the liabilities and responsibilities of all parties.

8. Review the bank's policies with respect to third-party transactions, and determine their reasonableness.

9. For transactions involving the Federal Reserve bank and other due from bank accounts, confer with the examiner assigned "Due from Banks," and determine the propriety of any outstanding funds transfer items.

10. Review the funds transfer activities report for the number of items received and the number of items paid over CHIPS, and FedWire to determine whether the volume of transactions on each of the systems is unusually large relative to the size of the bank. If the bank is a settling participant in CHIPS, review the list of non-settling participant and total amount settled for each.

11. Review suspense or adjustment accounts for any unusual items, abnormal fluctuations, or evidence of inefficient operation. Determine that they agree with departmental control totals and to the general ledger.

12. Review income and expense accounts related to wire transfer operations for frequency of entries caused by inaccurate execution of transfer requests. Show the total expenses incurred during the last calendar year and year-to-date for failing to make payments as instructed by bank customers.

13. By observing space and personnel allocated to the wire transfer area and location of communications terminals, determine whether existing conditions are adequate to provided security.

14. Determine compliance with laws, rulings, and regulations pertaining to the wire transfer area by:

    a. Reviewing previously obtained material and comparing it to Federal Reserve Regulation J, subpart B (12 CFR 210).

    b. Analyzing compliance with the record retention requirements of 31 CFR 103.33, 103.34, and 103.36 by:

        • Determining whether the bank maintains a record of advices, requests, or instructions given to an other domestic financial institution regarding a transaction intended to result in the transfer of funds of more that $10,000 to a person, account, or place outside the United States for a period of five years.

        • Determining whether the bank retains an original or copy of documents granting signature authority over wire transfers from deposit accounts for a period of five years.

15. Discuss with appropriate officer(s), and prepare summaries in appropriate report form of:

    a. Internal control exceptions and deficiencies in, or non- compliance with, written policies, practices, and procedures.

    b. Uncorrected audit deficiencies.

    c. Violations of law, rulings, and regulations.

    d. The level of understanding by supervisory officers of definitions, terminology, operating arrangements, accounting procedures, and time limitations concerning wire transfer operations.

e. The operating efficiency and physical security of the bank's wire transfer operation.

f. Adequacy of controls over settlement and credit risk exposure.

g. Recommended corrective action when policies, practices, or procedures are deficient.

16. Prepare a memorandum, and update work programs with any information that will facilitate future examinations.

Payment Systems and
Funds Transfer Activities
(Section 410)   Internal Control Questionnaire

Review the bank's internal controls, policies, practices, and procedures regarding funds transfer activities. The bank's system should be documented in a complete, concise manner and should include, where appropriate, narrative descriptions, flowcharts, copies of forms used, and other pertinent information.

This questionnaire is designed in two separate modules. Module A is intended to be used as a review of operations and internal controls and should be applied in every institution to each wire transfer operation. Module B is intended to be used by examiners in their evaluations of accounting methods and controls related to overdrafts, advances against uncollected or anticipated deposits, and settlement risk. Although the concepts contained in Module B are universally applicable, it is intended to be used only in institutions which participate in one or more of the true funds transfer systems (i.e., FedWire, and CHIPS).

Module A

Organization and Management of Funds Transfer Function

Organization

1.   Has a current organization plan been developed that shows the structure of the funds transfer function?

2.   Does senior management provide administrative direction for operations of the funds transfer function?

3.   Does management regularly review staff compliance with credit and personnel procedures, operating instructions, and internal controls?

4.   Does management receive and review activity and quality control reports?

5. Are those reports designed to show unusual activity or disclose system use without proper authorization?

6. Is management informed of new systems design and available hardware for the wire transfer system?

Personnel

7. Has the institution taken steps to ensure that screening procedures are applied to personnel hired for sensitive positions in the wire transfer area?

8. Does the institution prohibit new employees from working in sensitive areas of the wire transfer function?

9. Is special attention paid by supervisory staff to new employees assigned to work in the wire transfer function?

10. Are temporary employees excluded from working in sensitive areas? If not, is the number of such employees limited?

11. Are statements of indebtedness required of employees in sensitive positions of the wire transfer function?

12. Are employees subject to unannounced rotation of responsibilities, regardless of the size of the institution?

13. Are relatives of employees in the wire transfer function precluded from working in the same institution's bookkeeping or data processing departments?

14. Does the institution's policy require that employees take a minimum number of consecutive days as part of their annual vacation?

15. Is the institution's vacation policy being enforced?

16. Does management reassign employees who have given notice of

resignation or been given termination notices from sensitive areas of the wire transfer function?

17. Is a training program used to alert personnel to the current trends in wire transfer activities and to the necessity of adequate internal control?

Operating Procedures

18. Do written procedures exist for employees in the incoming, preparation, data entry, balance verification, transmission, accounting, reconciling, and security areas of the wire transfer function?

19. Do the procedures cover:

   a. Access to the wire transfer area and user files?

   b. Terminal security and password control?

   c. Control over test words, signature lists, and opening and closing messages?

   d. Origination of wire transfer transactions and the modification and deletion of payment orders or messages?

   e. Review of rejected payment orders or messages?

   f. Verification of sequence numbers?

   g. End-of-day accounting for all transfer requests and message traffic?

   h. Control over messages or payment orders received too late to process the same day?

   i. Control over payment orders with future value dates?

   j. Retention of unbroken monitor roll?

   k. Supervisory review of all adjustments, reversals, reasons for reversals, and open items?

l. Contingency planning?

20. Are those procedures periodically reviewed and updated?

Agreements

21. Are agreements concerning wire transfer operations between the financial institution and its hardware and software vendors, maintenance companies, customers, correspondent banks, and the Federal Reserve bank in effect and current? (Agreements with the Federal Reserve bank should specifically refer to the operating circular(s) regarding wire transfer of funds pursuant to subpart B of Regulation J.)

22. Do the agreements fix responsibilities and accountability between the parties?

23. Do both the hardware and software vendors guarantee continuity of service in the event of a failure? If so, does the guarantee specify recovery time?

24. Are there agreements between the financial institution and vendors setting forth the vendors' liability for actions performed by their employees?

Contingency Plans

25. Have written contingency plans been developed for partial or complete failure of the systems and/or communication lines between the financial institution and the New York Clearing House, Federal Reserve bank, data centers, and/or service companies?

26. Are those contingency plans reviewed regularly?

27. Are those plans tested periodically?

28. Has management distributed those plans to all wire transfer personnel?

29. Are sensitive information and equipment adequately secured before evacuation in an emergency, and is further access to the affected areas denied by security personnel?

Operations

Processing

30. Are all incoming and outgoing payment orders and message requests received in the wire transfer area, and are payment orders:

    a. Time stamped or sequentially numbered for control?

    b. Logged?

    c. Reviewed for signature authenticity?

    d. Reviewed for test verification, if applicable?

    e. Reviewed to determine whether personnel who initiate funds transfer requests have the authority to do so?

31. Are current lists of authorized signatures maintained in the wire transfer area?

32. Do those lists indicate the amount of funds which the individuals are authorized to release?

33. Are payment orders and message requests reviewed by someone other than the receipt clerk for:

    a. Propriety of the transactions?

    b. Future dates, especially for multiple transaction requests?

34. Are the receipt, data entry, and authentication functions in the wire transfer area adequately segregated?

35. Are all transactions checked by a supervisor prior to release of the payments?

36. Are all payment orders and message requests accounted for in an end-of-day proof to ensure that all requests have been processed?

37. Are all pre-numbered forms, including cancellations, accounted for in the end-of-day proof?

38. Does the wire transfer department prepare a daily reconcilement of funds sent and received over the system (CHIPS and FedWire) indicating the dollar amount and number of transactions?

39. Is the daily reconcilement of funds transfer and message request activity reviewed by supervisory personnel?

40. Are customer transfer and message requests that have been rejected by an in-house terminal carefully controlled and assigned a sequence number for accountability?

41. Are "as of" adjustments, open items, and reversals reviewed and approved by an officer?

42. Do records of funds transfer message requests contain:

    a. A sequence number?

    b. An amount, if funds are to be paid?

    c. The name of the customer making the request?

    d. A date?

    e. A test code authentication, if funds are to be paid?

    f. Paying instructions?

g. Authorizing signatures for certain types and dollar amounts of transfers?

43. Does the flow of work proceed in a one-way direction to provide an adequate internal control environment?

44. Are all rejects and/or exceptions reviewed by someone not involved in the receipt, preparation, or transmittal of funds?

45. If the institution accepts transfer requests after the close of business or transfer requests with a future value date, are they properly controlled and processed?

46. Does the institution maintain adequate records as required by the Currency and Foreign Transactions Reporting Act of 1970 (also known as the Bank Secrecy Act)?

Testing

47. Are test codes used for telephonic requests for wire transfer transactions?

48. Are test codes used for transactions verified by someone other than the person who receives the request?

49. Are those codes restricted to authorized personnel?

50. Are those test codes maintained in a secure environment when not in use?

51. Is the testing area physically separated from the remainder of the operation?

Physical Security

52. Is access to the wire transfer area restricted to authorized personnel?

53. Are visitors to the wire transfer area required to:

a. Be identified?

b. Sign in?

c. Continuously display identification?

d. Be accompanied at all times?

54. Are personnel who are permitted entry to the operating area properly identified and required to continuously display identification?

55. Is written authorization given to those employees who remain in the wire transfer area after normal working hours? Who gives such authority? Are security guards informed?

56. Are the terminals controlled by key lock or password protected to prevent unauthorized access?

57. Are terminals in the wire transfer area regulated by:

a. Automatic time-out controls?

b. Time-of-day controls?

58. Are terminals and other hardware in the wire transfer area shut down after normal working hours?

59. Is terminal operator training conducted in a manner that will not jeopardize the integrity of live data or memo files?

60. Are passwords suppressed when entered in terminals?

61. Are operator passwords frequently changed? If so, how often?

62. Do correcting and reversing entries, as well as overrides, require supervisory approval?

63. Is supervisory approval required for terminal access made at other than

authorized times?

64. Are passwords restricted to different levels of access, such as data files and transactions, that can be initiated?

65. Are employees prohibited from taking keys for sensitive equipment out of the wire transfer area?

Module B

Supervision by Directors and Senior Management

1. Are the directors and senior management kept informed about the nature and magnitude of the risks in the funds transfer activity?

2. Has the board of directors and/or senior management reviewed and approved any limits relating to the risks in the funds transfer activities? If so, when were the limits last reviewed?

3. Is senior management and/or the board of directors advised of customers with:

   a. Large intraday and overnight overdrafts? If so, are other extensions of credit to the same customers combined to show the total credit exposures?

   b. Large drawings against uncollected funds?

4. Is senior management and/or the board of directors, under established policies and procedures, required to review at predetermined frequencies:

   a. The volume of transactions, the creditworthiness of customers, and the risks involved in the funds transfer activity?

   b. Credit and other exposures related to safe and sound banking practices?

c. The capabilities of the staff and the adequacy of the equipment relative to current and expected volume?

5. Are there periodic credit reviews of funds transfer customers?

6. Are the reviews adequately documented?

7. Are the reviews conducted by competent credit personnel independent of account and operations officers?

8. Does the institution make payments in anticipation of the receipt of covering funds? If so, are such payments approved by officers with appropriate credit authority?

9. Are intraday exposures limited to amounts expected to be received the same day?

10. Have customer limits been established for FedWire and CHIPS exposure which include consideration of intraday and overnight overdrafts?

11. Are groups of affiliated customers included in such limits?

12. Do the limits appear to be reasonable in view of the institution's capital position and the creditworthiness of the respective customers?

13. How often are the limits reviewed and updated?

14. Are the customer limits reviewed by senior management? How frequently?

15. Are intraday overdraft limits established in consideration of other types of credit facilities for the same customer?

16. Are payments in excess of established limits approved on the basis of information indicating that covering funds are in transit to the financial institution? If so, who is authorized to make such approvals?

17. Are payments against uncollected funds and intraday overdrafts in excess

of established limits referred to a person with appropriate credit authority for approval before releasing payments?

18.   If payments exceed the established limits, are steps taken promptly to obtain covering funds?

Accounting, Records, and Controls

19.   Does the institution receive cables or other advices from its customers indicating amounts to be paid and received and the source of covering funds?

20.   If the detail of receipts is not received, is the institution advised by its customers of the total amount to be received for the day?

21.   Is this information maintained and followed for exceptions?

22.   Is an intraday posting record kept for each customer showing opening collected and uncollected balances, transfers in, transfers out, and the collected balance at time payments are released?

23.   Are significant CHIPS or FedWire payments and receipts by other departments of the institution on behalf of a customer communicated to a monitoring unit promptly during the day to provide adequate information on each customer's overall exposure?

24.   Does the demand deposit accounting system give an accurate collected funds position?

25.   Have limits been established within which a designated person may authorize release of payments after reviewing the activity of the customer? Is a record of approvals of such releases maintained by the institution?

26.   When an overnight overdraft occurs, is a determination made as to whether a fail caused the overdraft? If so, is this properly documented? Is adequate follow-up made to obtain the covering funds in a timely manner?

27. Does the institution have a record of payments it failed to make promptly?

28. Is the record reviewed to evaluate the efficiency of the department?

29. Is corrective action initiated when appropriate?

30. Are investigations and follow-ups for failed payments conducted by personnel independent of the operating unit?

31. Do credit advices sent to customers clearly indicate that credits to their accounts received through CHIPS are conditional upon final settlement at the end of the day?

32. For the settling institutions on CHIPS, are the net debit positions of the non-settling participants relayed to appropriate personnel as soon as they become known?

33. Who is responsible for verifying that respondents' net debit positions are covered the same day?

34. Are the follow-up procedures adequate to facilitate the receipt of funds?

35. Is senior management required to make decisions to refuse to cover a net debit settlement position of a respondent?

36. Has the institution devised and maintained an adequate system of internal accounting controls as required by the Foreign Corrupt Practices Act of 1977?

Conclusion

1. Is the foregoing information an adequate basis for evaluating internal control in that there are no significant additional internal auditing procedures, accounting controls, administrative controls, or other circumstances that impair any controls or mitigate any weaknesses indicated above (explain negative answers briefly, and indicate

conclusions as to their effect on specific examination or verification procedures)?

2.   Based on a composite evaluation, as evidenced by answers to the foregoing questions, internal control is considered _____ (good, medium, or bad).

1. Balance incoming transfer requests to completed transaction tickets.

2. Using appropriate sampling techniques, select wire transfer messages from bank records, and:

    a. Determine that messages or transfer requests that require test codes or signature verification are properly authenticated.

    b. Determine that tickets supporting incoming and outgoing transfer requests agree with entries posted to the Federal Reserve bank, correspondent banks, and customer's accounts.

    c. Determine that a proper explanation has been recorded and approved for rejected or unprocessed messages.

    d. Review funds transfer messages and determine if those transfers were initiated within individual lines of authority.

    e. Review, for content, transfer requests forms supporting wire transfer messages. Check to see that the forms contain, at a minimum:

        • The name of the person, firm, or bank making the request (also specific transferor).
        • The test code authentication (if applicable).
        • The amount.
        • The date.
        • Paying instructions.
        • The sequence number (or space for).

    f. Review any income and expense items related to the sampled messages, and trace the offsetting entries to bank or other customer accounts.

3.   Review signature cards and test key files, and determine if they contain information on inactive or closed customer accounts.

4.   Select items from suspense or adjustment accounts, and determine their authenticity.

5.   Select overdraft items, and determine that appropriate credit approval was obtained and payments were released within authorized intraday and/or overnight lending limits.

6.   Review any payments released in excess of established limits to ensure that proper approvals were made by officers with sufficient lending authority.

Payment System Risk Reduction Program —
Self-Assessment Review

Creditworthiness

A. Primary Factors

1. Asset Quality

   In determining the institution's asset quality self-assessment rating, have management and the directorate considered the following:

   a. Comments from the latest supervisory examination report regarding asset quality and management effectiveness?
   b. Level, distribution, and severity of classified assets?
   c. The level and composition of nonaccrual and reduced rate assets?
   d. Loss history and adequacy of valuation reserves?
   e. Ability to foresee, administer, and correct problem credits?
   f. Concentrations?
   g. Other factors?

2. Capital Adequacy

   In determining the institution's capital self-assessment rating, have management and the directorate considered the following:

   a. Comments from the latest supervisory examination report?
   b. Capital guidelines established by regulators?
   c. Asset quality and off-balance sheet activity?
   d. Growth?
   e. Profitability?
   f. Other factors?

3. Earnings

   In determining the institution's earnings self-assessment rating, have management and the directorate considered the following:

a. Comments from the latest supervisory examination report?
b. Return on assets?
c. Quality of earnings?
d. Growth?
e. Asset quality?
f. Provisions for loan losses?
g. Tax considerations?
h. Interest rate sensitivity?
i. Earnings history?
j. Dividend requirements?
k. Capital adequacy?
l. Other factors?

For each primary factor:

1. Does the institution consider available peer group and other available data for institutions with similar operating characteristics, such as consumer lending or wholesale activities?

2. Do peer group comparisons generally support the self-assessment as follows:

    Excellent—performance consistently above the 75th percentile, with most key measures above the 90th percentile.

    Very Good—performance consistently above the 50th percentile, with most key measures above the 75th percentile.

    Adequate—performance consistently above the 25th percentile with most key measures near peer averages and no significant measures in the lowest 10th percentile or below standards set by supervisory authorities.

    Below Standard—performance measures consistently below average, with significant weakness in one or more key measures.

Assessment of Primary Factors

Based on a review of the primary factors, a level should be assigned by the institution and the examiner for each factor:

Asset Quality

Institution   Examiner

Institution	Examiner	
_____	_____	Excellent
_____	_____	Very Good
_____	_____	Adequate
_____	_____	Below Standard

Comments:_____

_____

Capital Adequacy

Institution	Examiner	
_____	_____	Excellent
_____	_____	Very Good
_____	_____	Adequate
_____	_____	Below Standard

Comments:_____

_____

Earnings

Institution	Examiner	
_____	_____	Excellent
_____	_____	Very Good
_____	_____	Adequate
_____	_____	Below Standard

Comments:_____

_____

For each primary factor:

1. Is the institution's self-assessment rating consistent with guidelines?

2. If the institution's self-assessment rating is not consistent with guidelines, has management developed sufficient data to support the

inconsistency?

3. If the inconsistency is not adequately supported, does management plan to reassess the rating?

B. Modifying Factors

1. Liquidity

    In determining the position of the institution's liquidity self-assessment modifiers, have management and the directorate considered:

    a. Comments from the latest supervisory examination report addressing liquidity and overall condition of the institution?
    b. Management controls and policies?
    c. Borrowing history?
    d. Adequacy of policies and procedures?
    e. Rate sensitivity?
    f. The institution's asset and liability structures?
    g. Off-balance sheet funding sources and needs?

2. Holding Company and Affiliates

    If applicable, in determining position of the institution's holding company and affiliates self-assessment modifier, have management and the directorate considered:

    a. Comments from the most recent supervisory inspection report?
    b. Factors relating to capital, asset quality and earnings of the holding company and/or affiliates?
    c. Management?

For each modifying factor:

1. Does the institution consider available peer group and other available data for institutions with similar operating characteristics, such as consumer lending or wholesale activities?

2. Does peer group comparison generally support the self-assessment?

Assessment of Modifying Factors

Based on a review of the modifying factors, a level should be assigned by the institution and the examiner for each factor:

Liquidity

Institution	Examiner		
_____	_____	(0)	Liquidity is neutral. (Generally means the institution has a stable funding base with a reasonable cushion of assets or untapped funding sources available to meet contingencies.)
_____	_____	(-)	Liquidity is negative. (Generally means the institution has a funding vulnerability and/or is experiencing or has experienced a deterioration in the normal funding base.)
_____	_____	(+)	Liquidity is positive. (Generally means the institution is extremely liquid and has demonstrated asset liquidity as well as sound liability policies.)

Comments:_____

_____

_____

Holding Company and Affiliates

Institution	Examiner		
_____	_____	(0)	Influence is neutral. (Generally means holding company was characterized as being in satisfactory condition at its most recent inspection.)
_____	_____	(-)	Influence is negative. (Generally means holding company may be experiencing or expecting significant losses at the parent or in its non-bank affiliates; debt service requirements necessitate high dividend payout ratios at depository institution subsidiaries and affiliates; and consolidated capital is substantially less than that of the subsidiary institutions.)
_____	_____	(+)	Influence is positive. (Generally means holding company has demonstrated record of active support.)

Comments:_____

_____

_____

For each modifying factor:

1.   Is the institution's self-assessment rating consistent with guidelines?

2.   If the institution's self-assessment rating assessment rating is not consistent with guidelines, has management developed sufficient data to support the inconsistency?

3.   If the inconsistency is not adequately supported, does management plan to reassess the rating?

C. Overall Assessment

When integrating the assessments of the primary and modifying factors, the following should be asked:

1.   Do procedures employed by management and directorate to determine the creditworthiness self-assessment appear reasonable?

2.   Are conclusions adequately documented?

Operational Controls, Policies, and Procedures

In addition to the operations activities examined in the section 410 procedures, the institution's monitoring positions for both itself and its customers will be assessed.

A. Monitoring Positions Relative to Net Debit Caps

1.   Average Daily Activity

The following table should be completed to reflect the institution's average daily volume on each system on which it participates:

	Average Daily Volume			
System	Dollars Sent	Percent of Total	Dollars Received	Percent of Total
CHIPS				
FEDWIRE				
OTHER	‾‾‾‾		‾‾‾‾	
TOTAL		100%		100%

    a. Does the institution update the table at a frequency consistent with its fluctuations in activity?

    b. Does the table correctly reflect current level of activity?

    c. Are all large dollar payments systems considered when completing the table?

2.   Monitoring Individual System

Check monitoring frequency currently employed:

System	Real Time	Periodic (Note freq.)	No Interim Monitoring
CHIPS			
FEDWIRE			
OTHER			

    a. Does the institution update the table at an acceptable frequency?

    b. Is the monitoring capability appropriate for the volume of funds transfer activity?

3.   Cross-System Monitoring

    a. Does the institution monitor its payments activities on a cross-system basis?

    b. At what frequency?

Real time monitoring _____
Periodic (note freq.) _____
No interim monitoring _____

   c. Is this information reflected in the self-assessment file?

   d. Does the information reflect current activity?

Rating

Using the information from steps 1 through 3, the institution should be rated according to the following guide:

_____	**Strong**	—95 percent of total dollars sent and received are monitored on a real time basis or at least every 15 minutes.
		—A cross-system calculation of the institution's net debit/credit position is computed and compared to established limits on a real time basis or at least every 30 minutes.
_____	**Satisfactory**	—80 percent of the total average daily dollars volume sent is monitored on a real time basis or at least every 30 minutes.
		—A cross-system calculation of the institution's net debit/credit position is computed and compared to established limits on a real time basis or at least every 15 minutes.
_____	**Unsatisfactory**	—Any other condition.

   a. Provide a brief discussion of the institution's monitoring system, specifically analyzing the appropriateness of the monitoring procedures in use for the volume and nature of the institution's wire transfer activity.

   b. Is the institution's self-assessment rating consistent with the guidelines?

   c. If the institution's self-assessment rating is not consistent with the guidelines, has management developed sufficient data to support the conclusions?

   d. If the inconsistency is not adequately supported, does management plan to reassess the rating?

B. Monitoring Customer Positions

		YES	NO
1.	Has the institution identified customers who regularly participate in a large volume of wire transfer activity or in frequent large wire transfers?	____	____
2.	Are criteria for placement of a name on the list reasonable?	____	____
3.	Can the institution monitor these accounts taking into account the source of significant transactions?	____	____
4.	Do the monitoring systems include the opening collected balance?	____	____
5.	Is there a system in place to up-date the customer's balance reflecting intraday activity?	____	____
	Is the frequency appropriate?	____	____
6.	Does the overall system for monitoring positions of customers cover:		
	a. All significant sources generating customer account entries?	____	____
	b. Total transactions over established dollar limits?	____	____
	c. Overdraft limits?	____	____
	d. Single transfer limits?	____	____
7.	Are daily transactions reports generated and reviewed?	____	____
8.	Have transactions limit guidelines been established?	____	____
	a. If yes, are guidelines reasonable?	____	____
	b. Do transaction limits include a $50 million par value size limit on secondary market book-entry FedWire transfers?	____	____
	c. Are guidelines reviewed regularly?	____	____
9.	Does the system halt any transaction in excess of the established limits until appropriate action is taken?	____	____
10.	If documentation of action taken with regard to over limit transactions reflects consistent exceptions attributed to a customer, is analysis of those accounts intensified?	____	____
11.	Is staff trained in exception procedures?	____	____
12.	Are exception reports generated and reviewed?	____	____
13.	Do exception reports reflect all activity in excess of transaction limits?	____	____
14.	Do internal or external audits review the funds transfer environment at least annually? (These reviews should conform to the standards established by the Bank Administration Institute and the Federal Financial Institution Examinations Council.)	____	____
15.	Are auditors independent?	____	____
16.	Do audit reports reflect weaknesses in physical controls?	____	____
17.	Are audit exception clearing procedures adequate?	____	____
18.	Does the institution frequently incur daylight overdrafts and send large transfers to affiliated banks?	____	____
	a. Are controls in place to ensure that these extensions of credit stay within approved lines?	____	____
	b. Have the limits been adhered to?	____	____
	c. Have over-limit extensions been approved at the appropriate level of management?	____	____
19.	Are transfers to affiliates:		
	a. Made pursuant to a written agreement?	____	____
	b. Approved by the board of directors?	____	____

Rating

The institution should be rated according to the following guide:

_____	Strong	—Responses to all of the above are positive and comprehensive customer monitoring is in force for both debits and credits on a real time basis or at least intervals of 15 minutes or less.
_____	Satisfactory	—Responses to all of the above are positive and comprehensive customer monitoring is in force all debit transactions greater than or equal to the monitoring threshold on a real time basis or at least intervals of 30 minutes or less.
_____	Unsatisfactory	—Any other condition.

a. Provide a brief discussion of the institution's monitoring system, specifically analyzing consistency between monitoring procedures in use and volume and nature of the institution's wire transfer activity.

b. Is the institution's self-assessment consistent with guidelines?

c. If the institution's self-assessment rating is not consistent with guidelines, has management developed sufficient data to support the inconsistency?

d. If the inconsistency is not adequately supported does management plan to reassess the rating?

C. Overall Rating for Operational Controls, Policies and Procedures

Utilizing the ratings determined in parts A and B above, an overall rating should be determined from the following table (circle rating that applies):

Monitoring Institution Positions	Monitoring Customer Positions and Controls	Overall Rating
Strong	Strong	Strong
Strong	Satisfactory	Satisfactory
Satisfactory	Strong	Satisfactory

Satisfactory	Satisfactory	Satisfactory
Unsatisfactory	Satisfactory	Unsatisfactory
Strong	Satisfactory	Satisfactory
Satisfactory	Unsatisfactory	Unsatisfactory

Final Operational Controls Rating is _____.

Credit Policies and Procedures

		YES	NO
1.	Does the institution have a board of directors' approved entries policy specifically addressing daylight overdrafts and bilateral net credit limits?	___	___
2.	Does the policy address any regular extension of intra-day credit to affiliates?	___	___
3.	Have customers' aggregate exposures been identified?	___	___
4.	Have aggregate customer limits been approved and established?	___	___
5.	Do monitoring systems identify usage in excess of approved facilities on a timely basis?	___	___
6.	Do reporting systems provide adequate information to support evaluations of credit usage?	___	___
7.	Does the institution have exception identification and approval systems which are tailored to the speed, volume, and size of credit approvals required by its payment system generated exposures?	___	___
8.	Are the institution's review systems geared to single out and take action on deteriorating risk situations?	___	___
9.	Are all controls and procedures reviewed and tested by the institution's internal auditors?	___	___
10.	Is adequate training available and required for operations, credit, and account officer staff responsible for monitoring the intra-day overdraft exposure system?	___	___

Rating

The institution should be rated according to the following guide:

| _____ | Acceptable | —All or most responses to the checklist are positive. |
| _____ | Unacceptable | —All or most of the responses to the checklist are negative. |

Explain compensating controls where responses are negative.

Overall Assessment

The three component evaluations can be combined into a single overall assessment using the following table:

Credit Policies and Procedures	Operational Controls, Policies and Procedures	Credit Worthiness	Overall Assessment
Satisfactory	Strong	Excellent	High Cap
		Very Good	Above Average Cap
		Adequate	Average Cap
		Below Standard	No Cap
Satisfactory	Satisfactory	Excellent or Very Good	Above Average Cap
		Adequate	Average Cap
		Below Standard	No Cap
Satisfactory	Unsatisfactory	Any	No Cap
Unsatisfactory	Any	Any	No Cap

www.ingramcontent.com/pod-product-compliance
Lightning Source LLC
Chambersburg PA
CBHW052017280526
45793CB00005B/1014